This book belongs to:

. . . . . . . . . . . . . . . . . . . . . . . . . . . . .

CAUTION: The handling of the scissors must always
take place under the supervision of an adult!

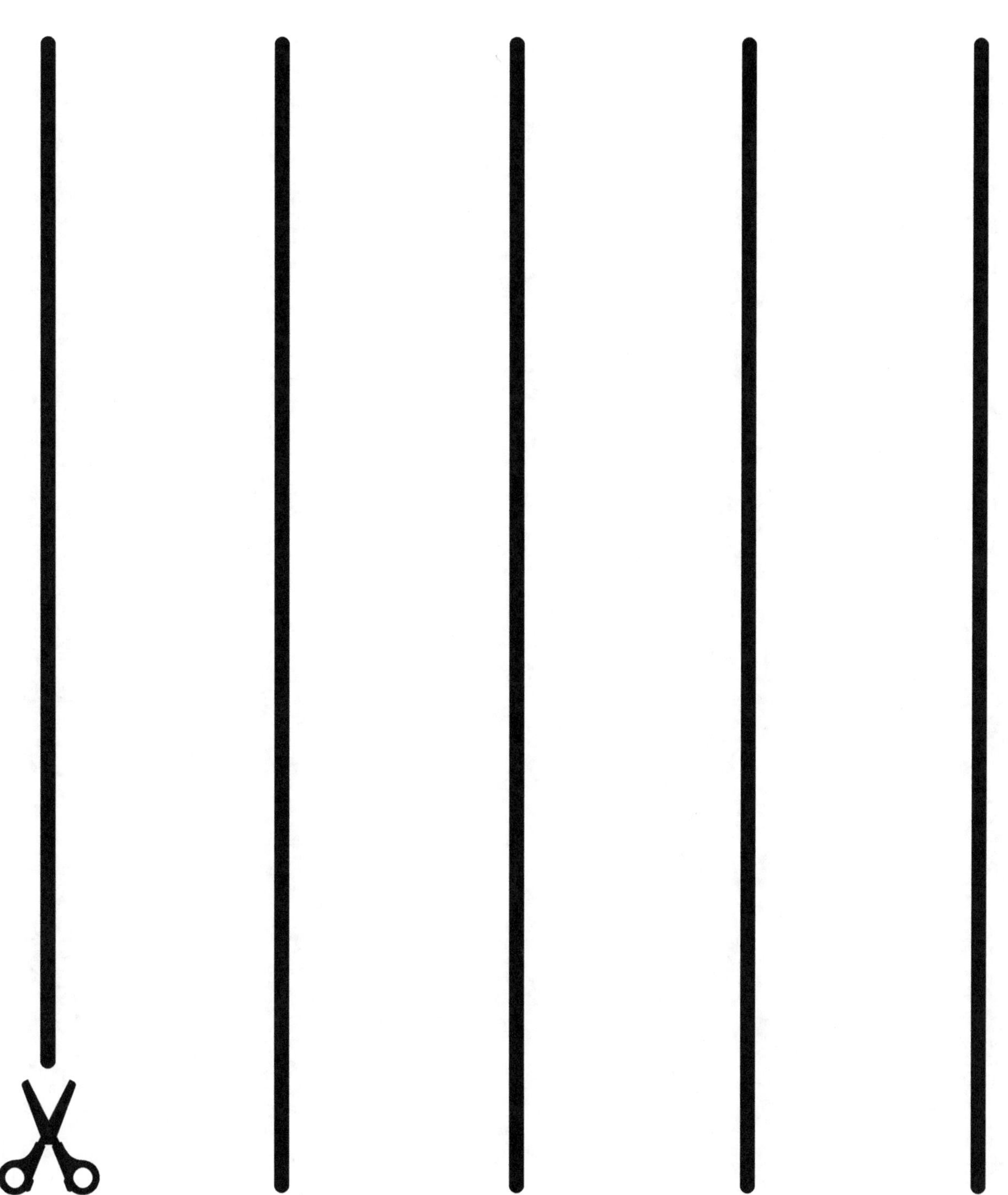

Cut along the lines.

# Cut along the lines.

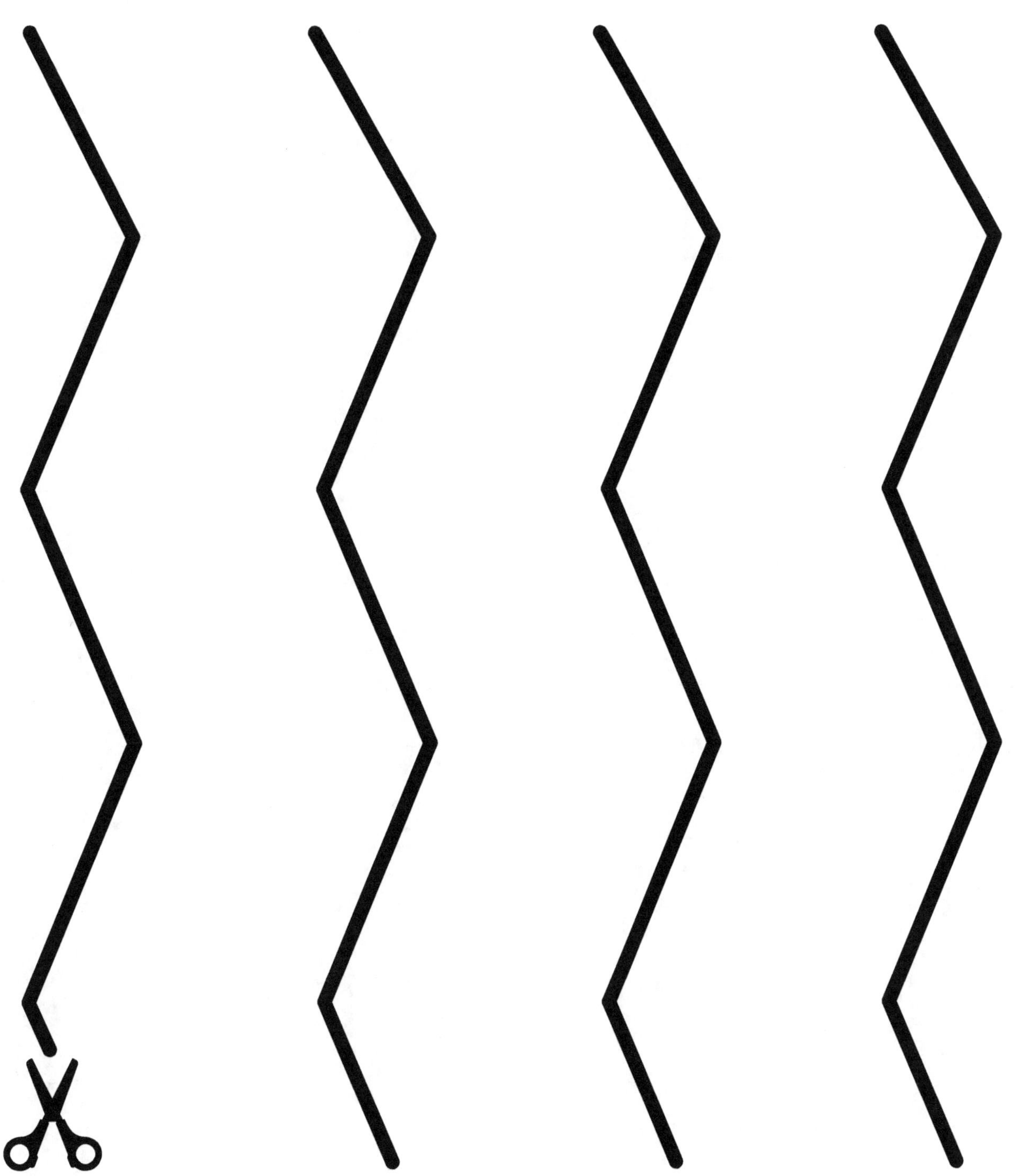

# Cut along the lines.

# Cut along the lines.

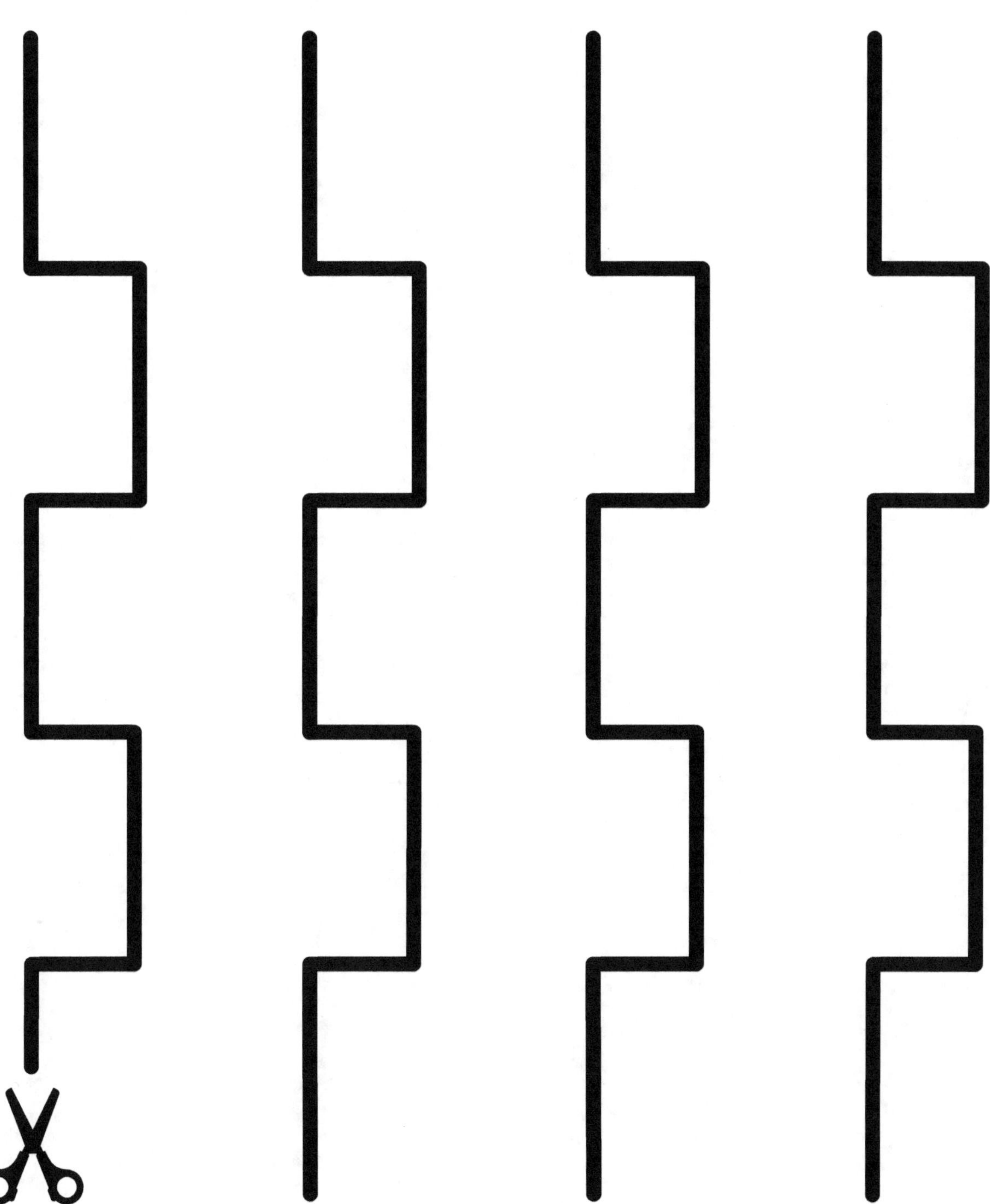

# Cut along the lines.

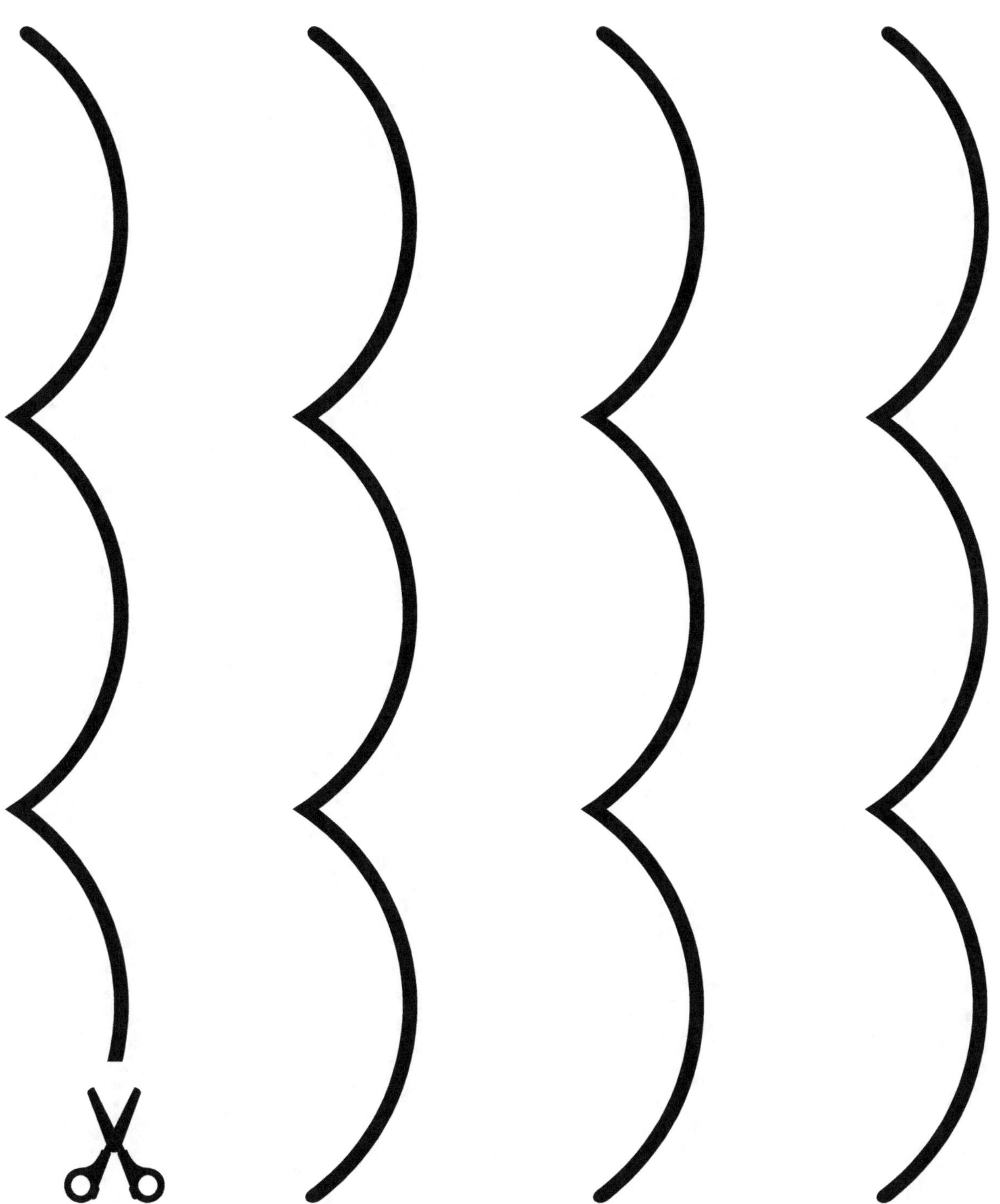

# Cut along the lines.

# Cut along the lines.

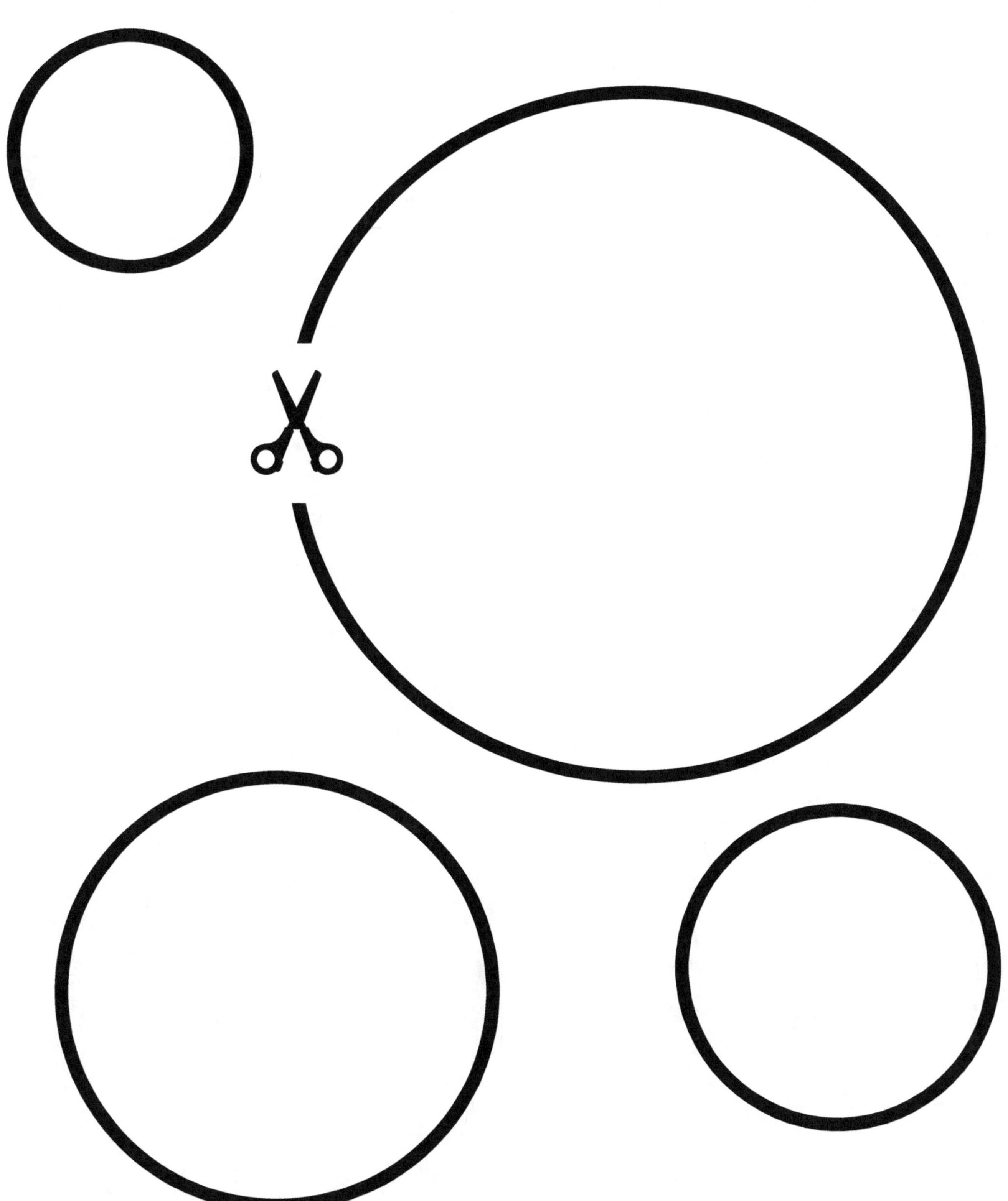

**Cut along the lines.**

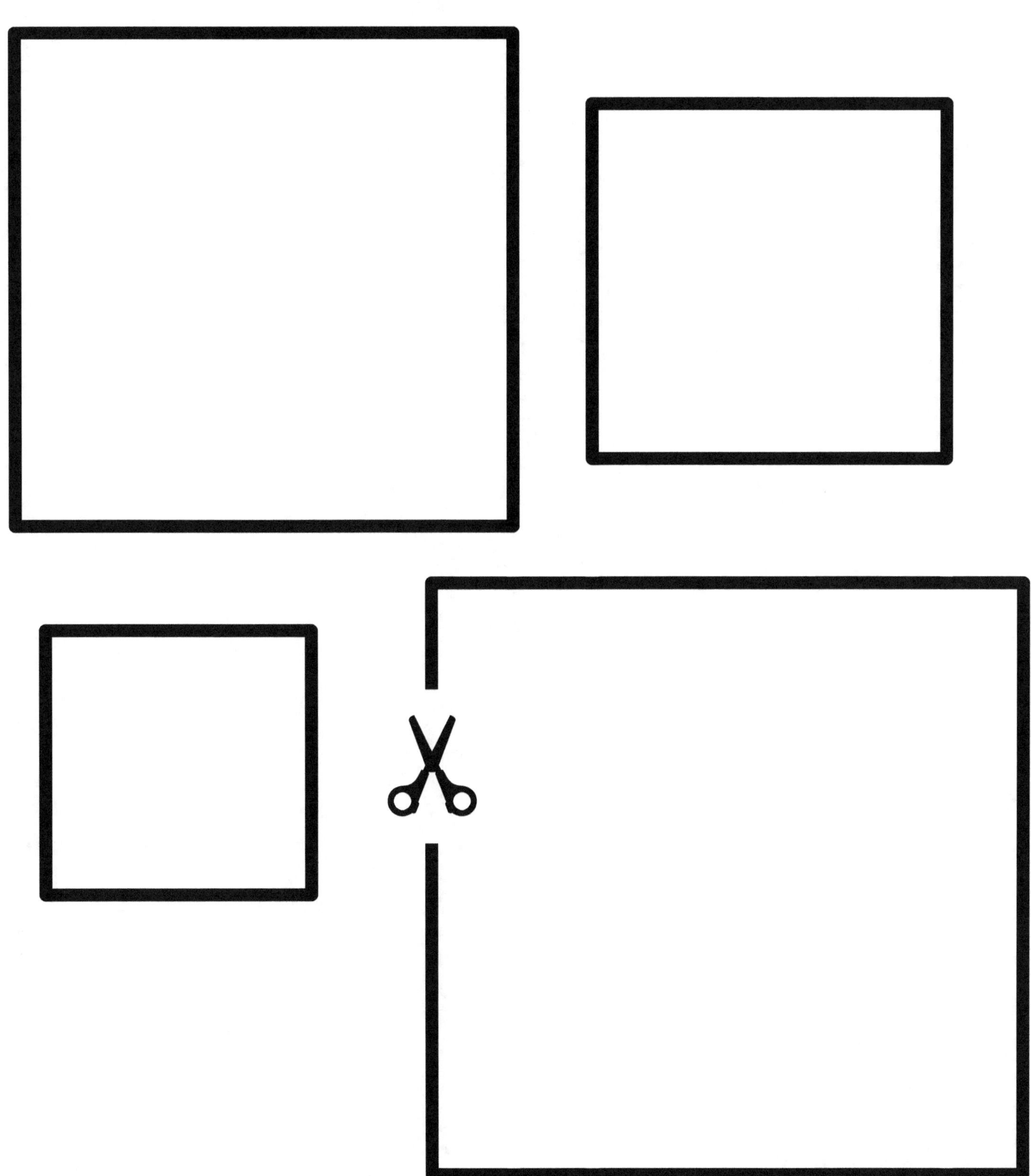

# Cut along the lines.

## Cut along the lines.

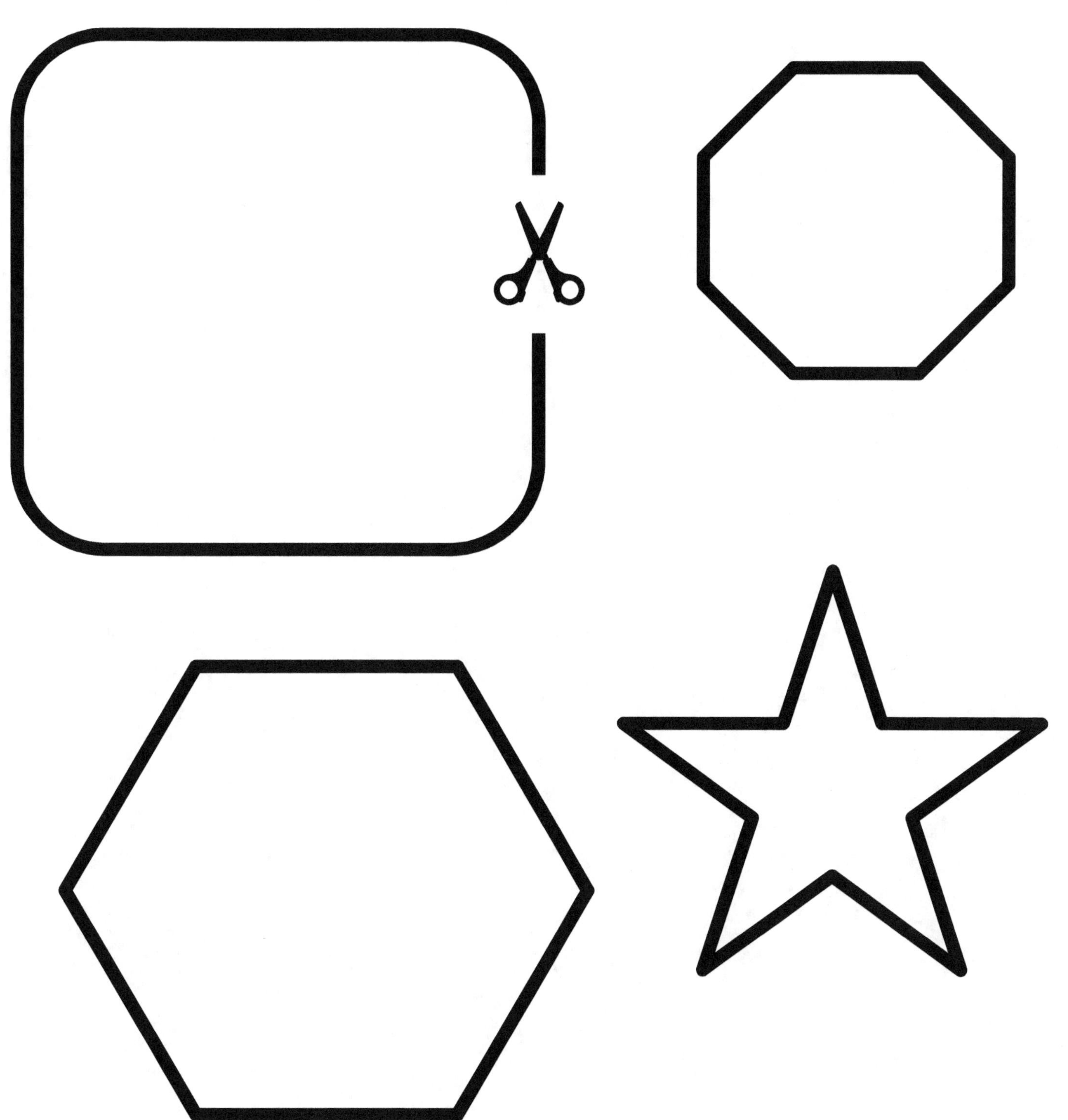

Cut along the lines.

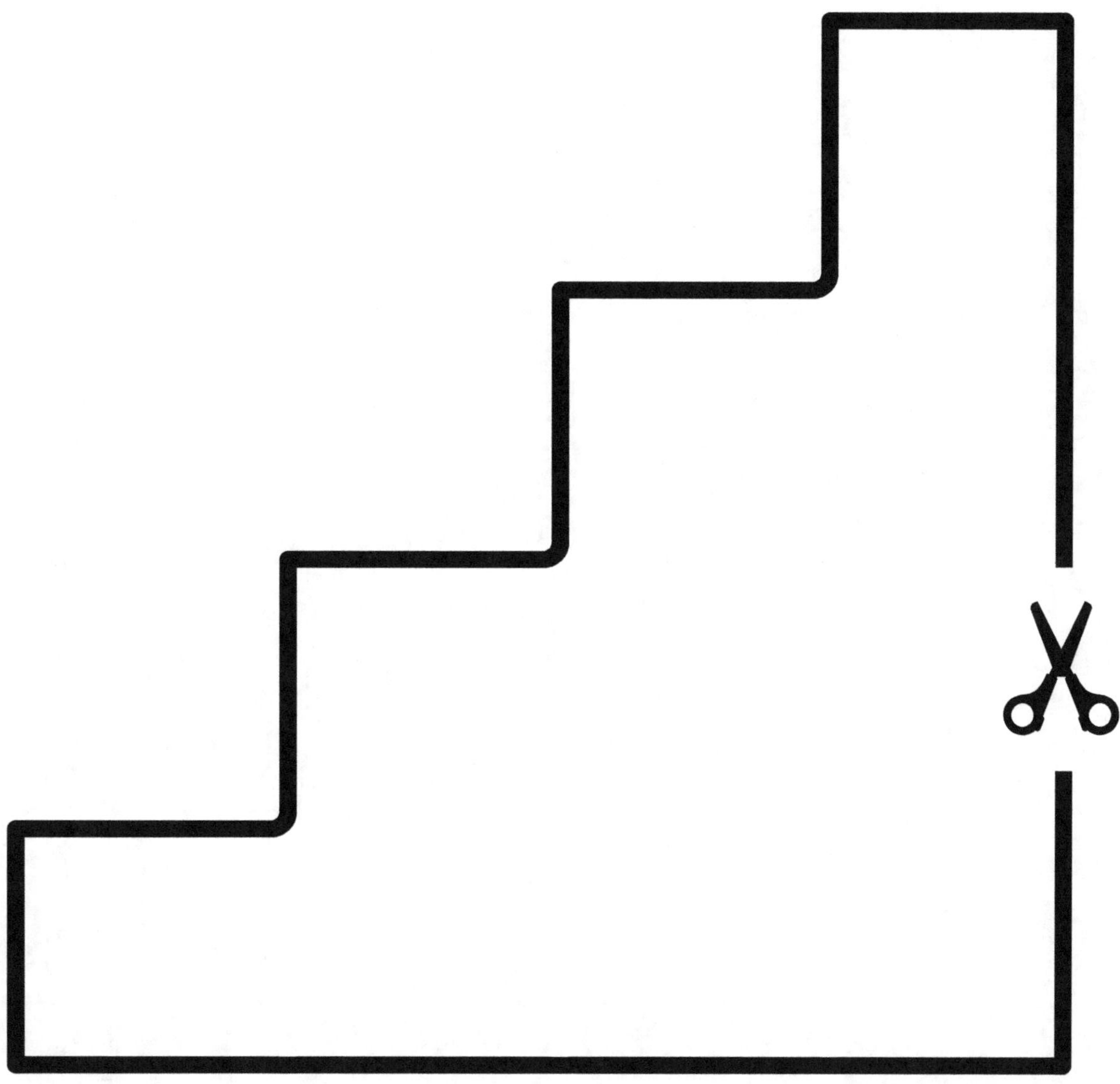

# Cut along the lines.

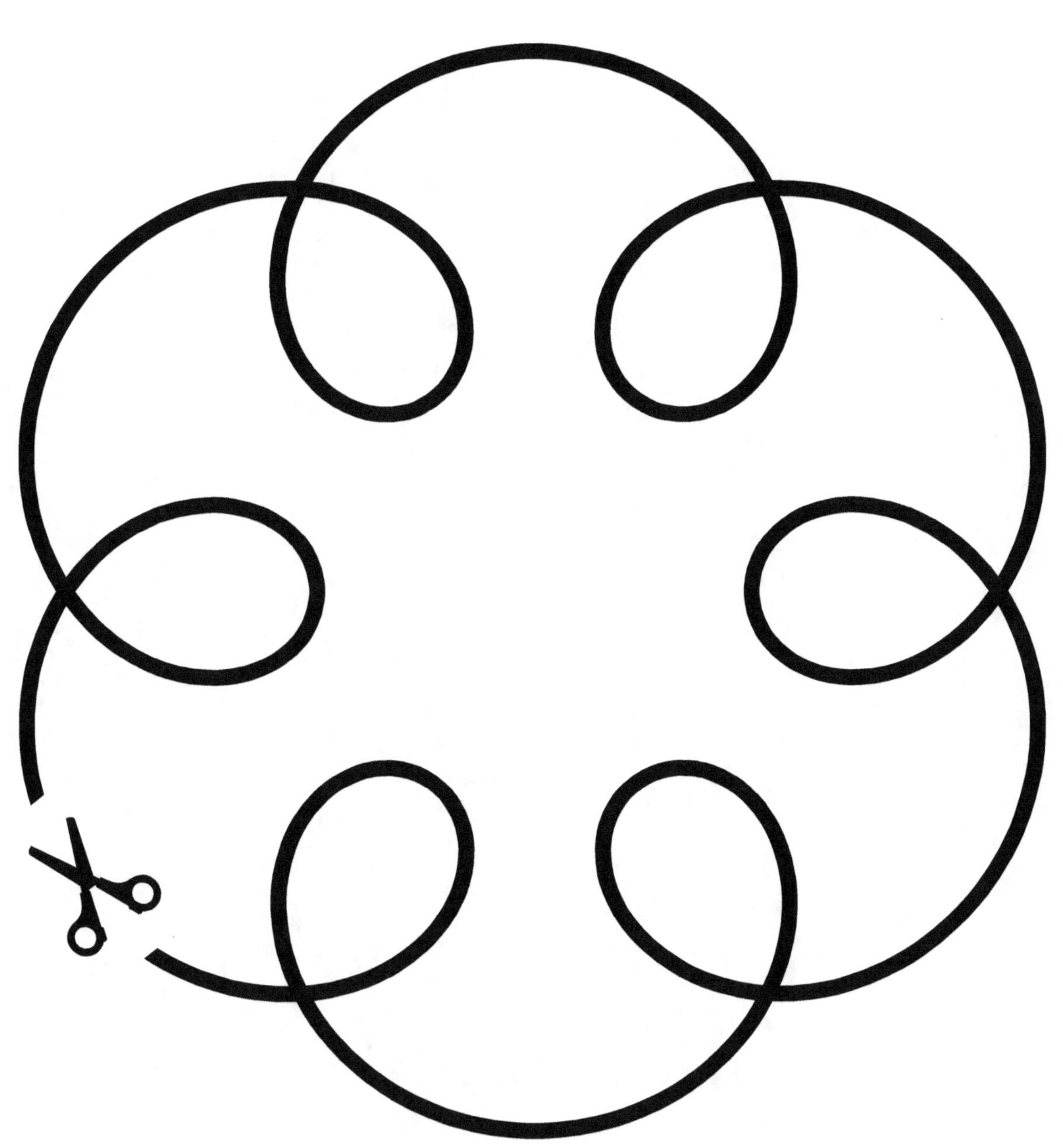

Cut along the lines.

# Cut along the dotted lines.

## Cut along the dotted lines.

Give the heart
to someone
special for you.

# Cut along the dotted lines.

## Cut along the dotted lines.

# Cut along the dotted lines.

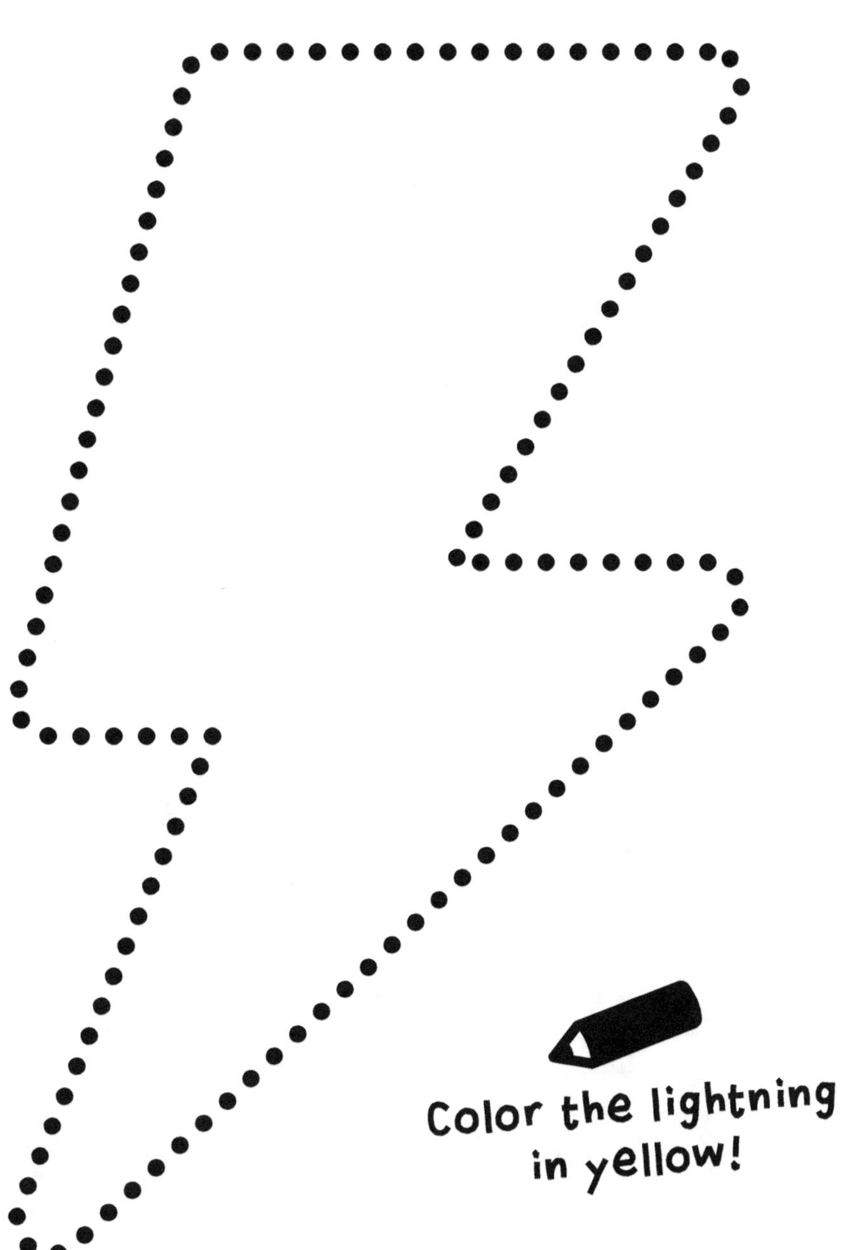

Color the lightning
in yellow!

**Cut along the dotted lines.**

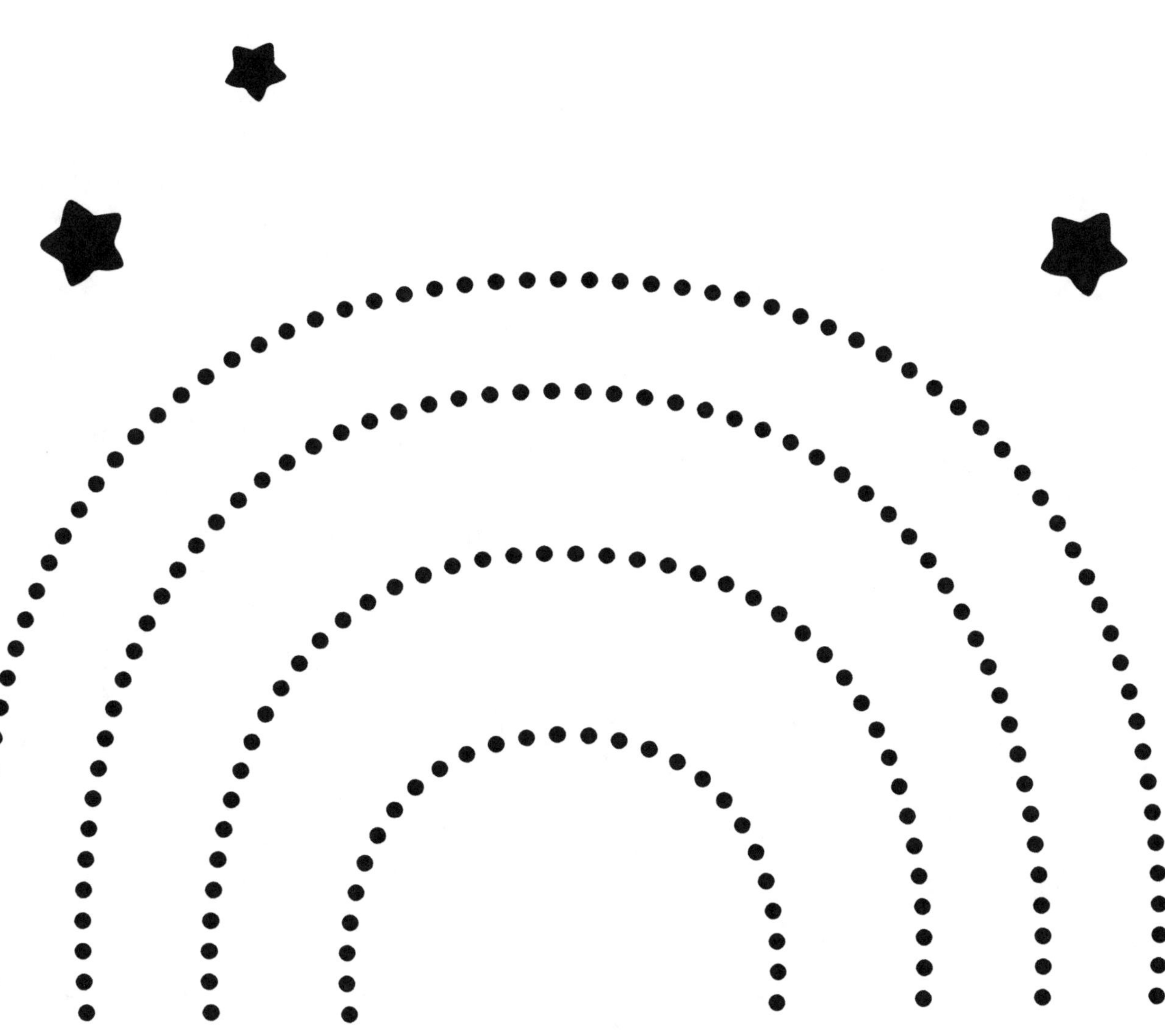

# Cut along the dotted lines.

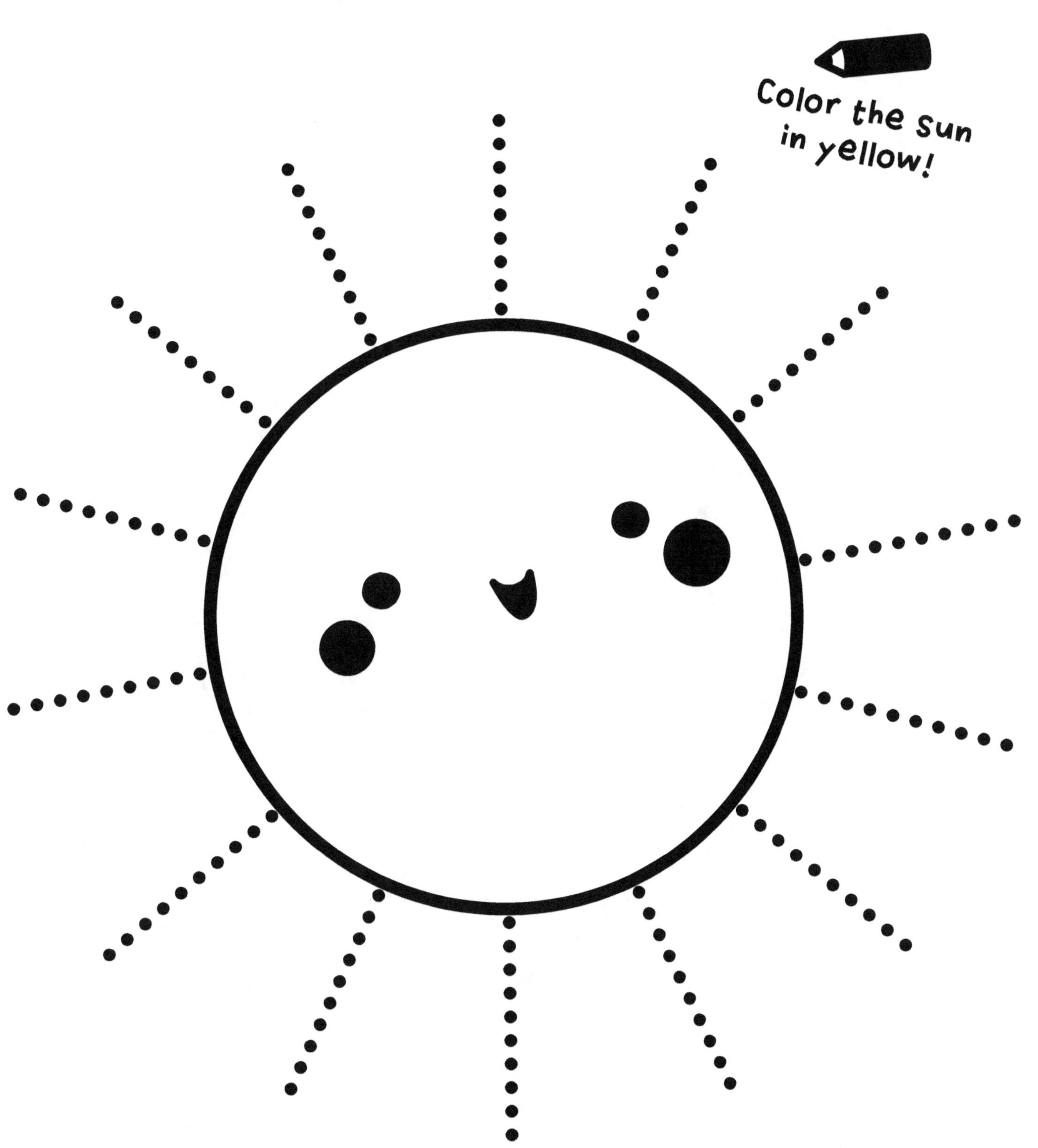



Cut along the dotted lines.

# Cut along the dotted lines.

# MOON

**Cut along the dotted lines.**

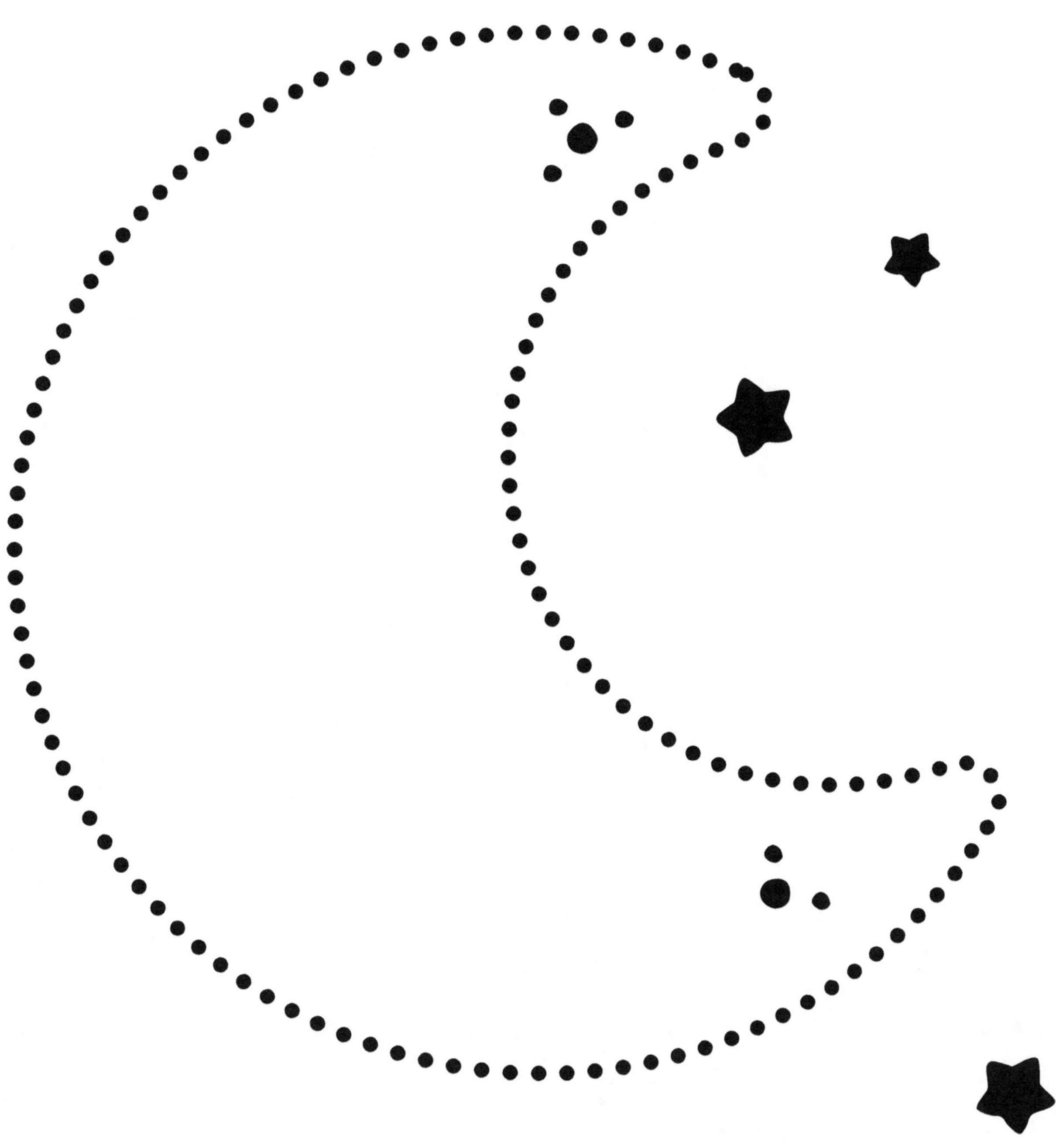

Cut along the dotted lines.

ROCKET

Cut along the dotted lines.

## Cut along the dotted lines.

Color the apple
in green !

**Cut along the dotted lines.**

Color the pear
with the color
of your choice !

## Cut along the dotted lines.

Color the strawberry in red!

# Cut along the dotted lines.

Cut along the dotted lines.

Cut along the dotted lines.

Cut along the dotted lines.

Cut along the dotted lines.

# MONKEY

**Cut along the dotted lines.**

Cut along the dotted lines.

Cut along the dotted lines.

WHALE

Cut along the dotted lines.

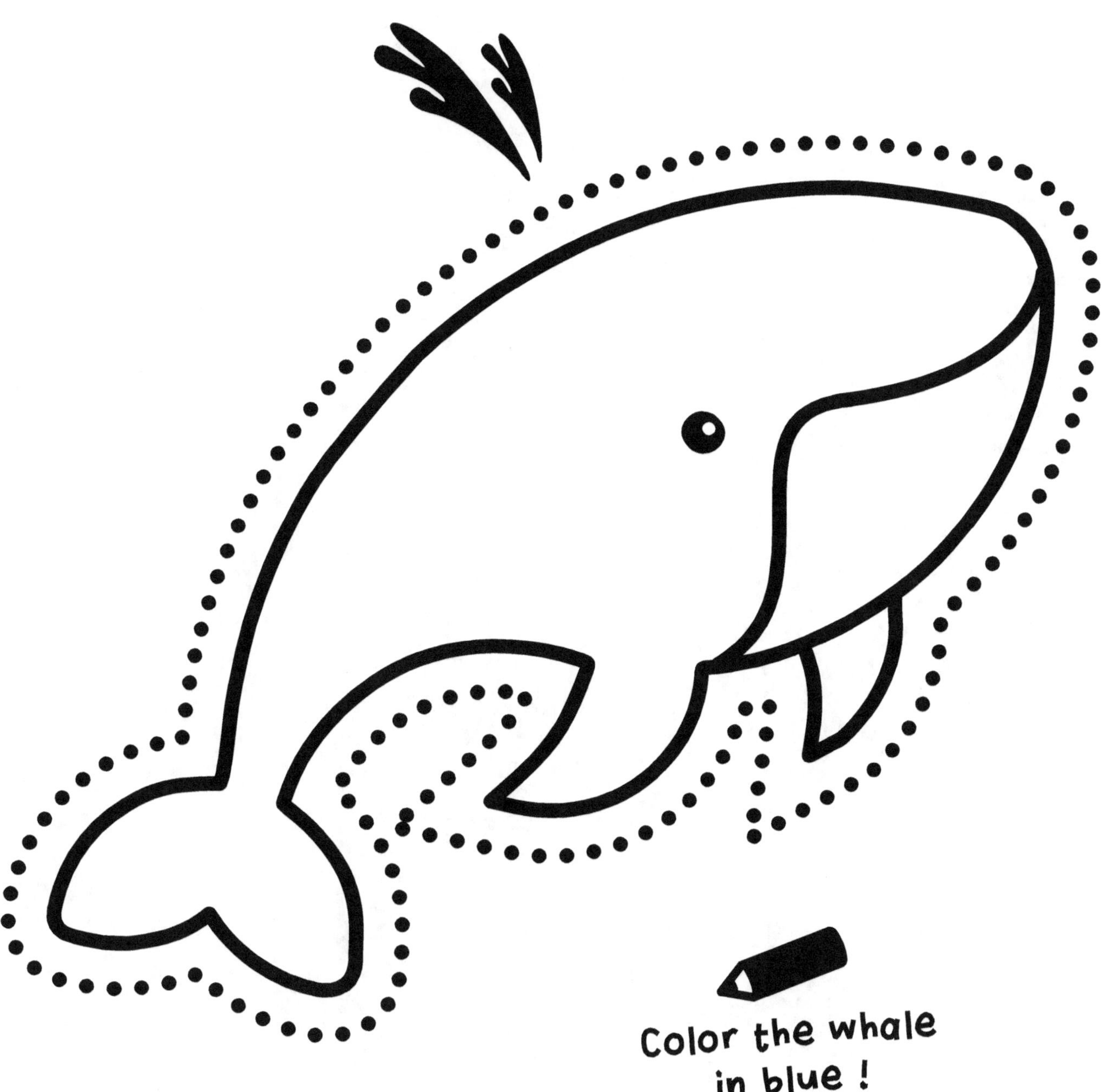

Color the whale
in blue !

# JELLYFISH

Cut along the dotted lines.

Cut along the dotted lines.

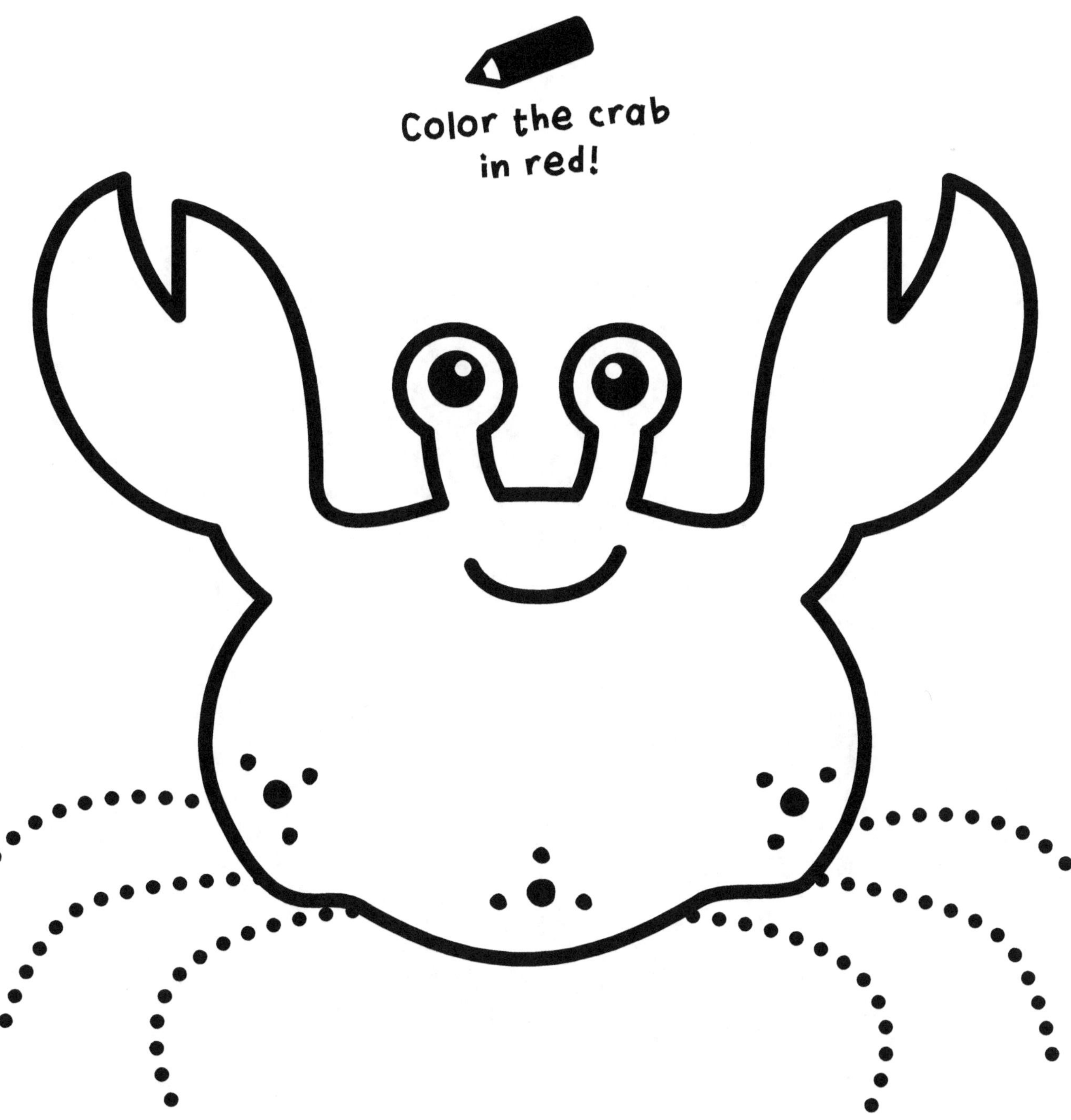


Cut along the dotted lines.

Cut along the dotted lines.

## Cut along the dotted lines.

SNAKE

Cut along the dotted lines.

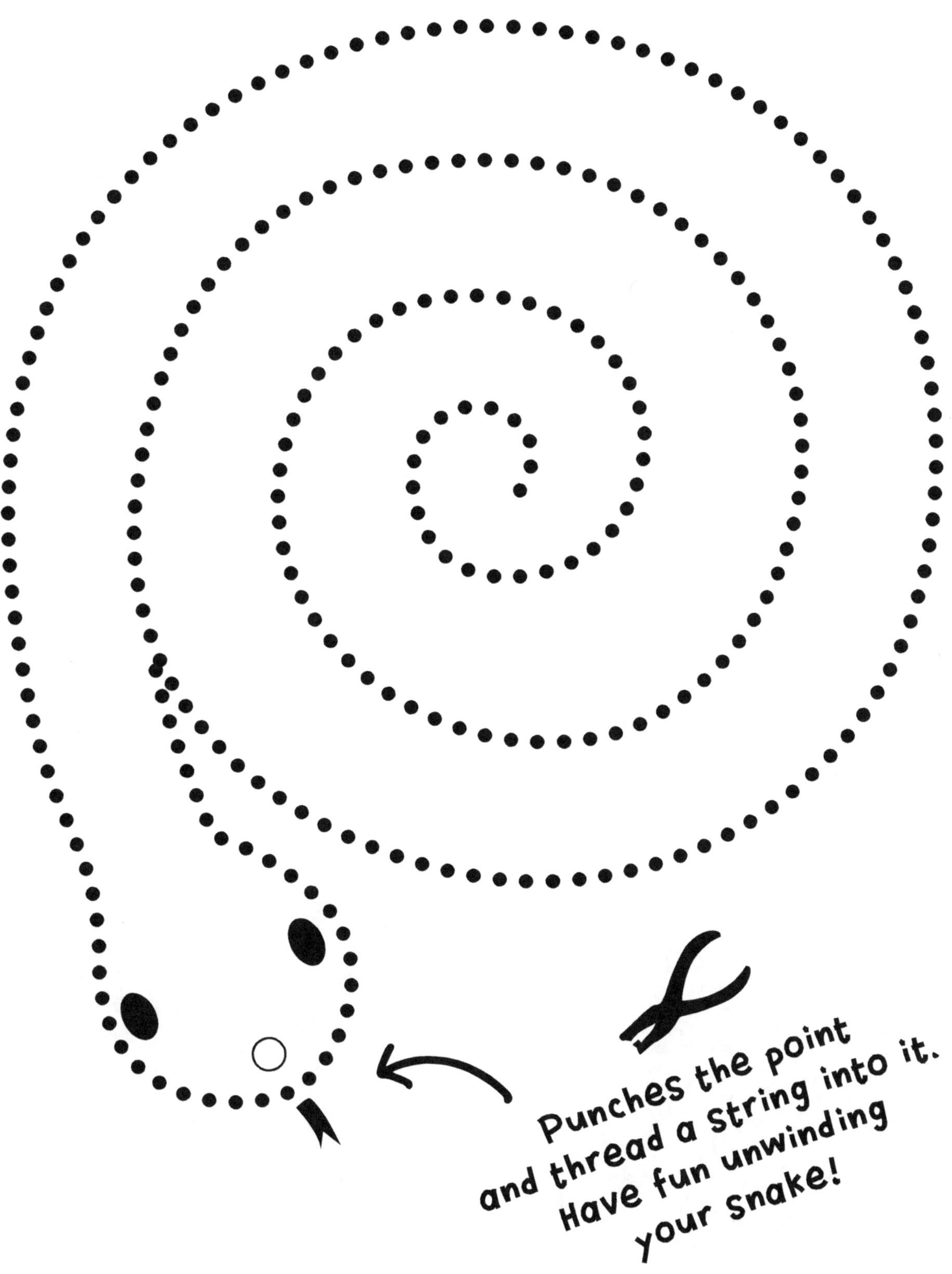

# Cut along the dotted lines.

Draw on your puzzle before cutting it!

Cut out dotted shapes
and glue them on the mushroom.

Cut out dotted shapes
and glue them on the pumpkin.

Cut out dotted apples
and glue them on the apple tree.

# TRUCK

Cut out the packages and glue them on the truck trailer.

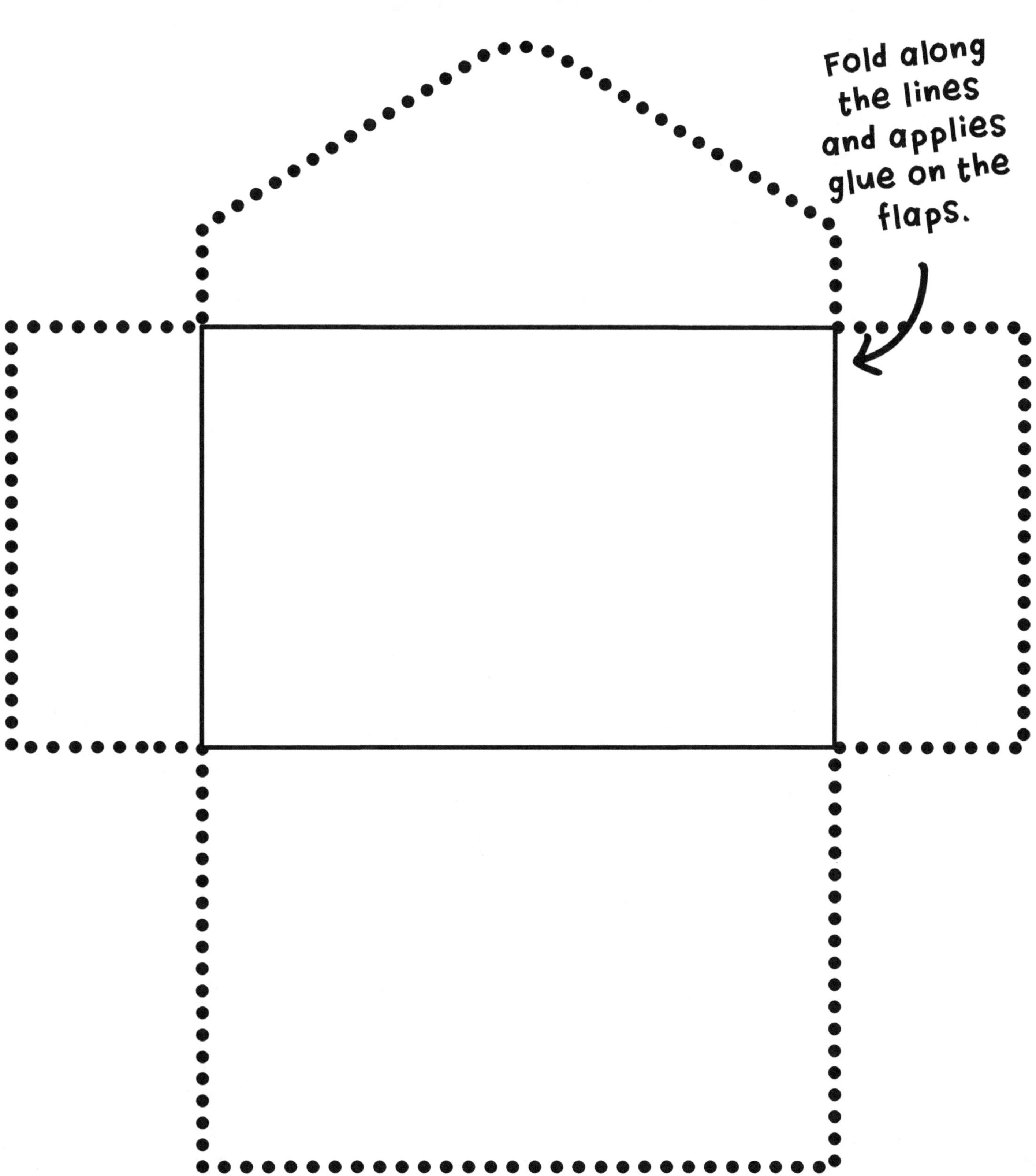

Cut along the dotted lines.
Fold along the lines and applies glue on the flaps.

www.ingramcontent.com/pod-product-compliance
Lightning Source LLC
LaVergne TN
LVHW080545200726
843508LV00008B/1499